The Sevenfold Awakening

Verses of the Seven Chakras

Dolma Pathela

BookLeaf Publishing

India | USA | UK

Dedication

To the Root that grounds us,
To the Flow that frees us,
To the Fire that drives us,
To the Heart that opens us.

To the Voice that speaks our truth,
To the Eye that sees beyond,
To the Crown that dissolves us into the infinite.

For the seekers, the healers, the ones who are learning to rise.
For the ones who are still remembering their own light.

This book is a journey through you—
through all that you are, all that you have been,
and all that you are becoming.

May it guide you home to yourself.

Preface

We are more than just bodies moving through time.
We are energy, flowing and shifting, expanding and
awakening.
Within us, seven centers of power—seven chakras—form
the bridge between the physical and the divine. They
hold our fears and desires, our voices and silences, our
roots and our wings. They are the story of what it means
to be human, yet limitless.

This book explores the seven energy centers, unfolding
like the petals of a lotus. Each part resonates with a
different chakra, guiding you from the depths of the
earth to the vastness of the cosmos. These words are not
meant to be read once and left behind. Let them sit with
you. Let them stir something ancient inside you. Let
them remind you of what you already know but may
have forgotten—that you are whole!

Acknowledgements

No journey is ever walked alone, and this book is no exception.

I am grateful for the ones who walk this path alongside me—friends, mentors, and kindred spirits—your presence is a light on this journey.

For the lessons that arrived disguised as challenges and the moments of stillness that revealed the most profound truths.

For those who have held space for my voice, encouraging me to speak, to feel, to create.

And for the universe itself— for whispering, for waiting, for awakening.

This book is not mine alone. It is woven from every experience, every soul, every breath that has shaped me.

Thank you.

Part I. Root Chakra (Muladhara) – The Foundation

Symbol: 4-petalled lotus, square, downward-facing triangle

Color: Red

Element: Earth

Location: Base of the spine

Function: Governs survival, stability, and grounding

Blocked Symptoms: Fear, insecurity, lack of purpose

Balanced State: Confidence, strength, stability, independence

Verses:

1.1 Roots of the Earth – *Finding belonging and ancestral wisdom.*

1.2 The Weight of Fear – *Confronting insecurity and learning trust.*

1.3 I Am Here – *Affirming stability and presence.*

1.1. Roots of the Earth

(Finding belonging and ancestral wisdom)

I was born from soil and sorrow,
a whisper carried on the winds of time.
The echoes of those before me hum
in the marrow of my bones,
teaching me the songs of survival.
Beneath my feet, the earth remembers—
stories pressed into rock and root,
promises buried like seeds,
waiting to bloom into knowing.
I am not alone.
I stand on the shoulders of those
who walked before,
their whispers anchoring me deeper,
their strength rising through my veins.
Their roots are my roots.
Their fire is my fire.
Their journey continues in me.
"I am home."

P.S.: Your roots are not just where you were born, but the wisdom you choose to inherit. Let them ground you, but never chain you.

1.2. The Weight of Fear

Fear curls around my spine,
a serpent whispering in my ear—
"You are not safe,
you are not enough,
you will never belong."
I have carried this weight too long,
bent beneath the burden of old wounds,
shadows of hands that once trembled,
voices that doubted before I could speak.
I breathe deep,
filling the hollow spaces within.
I let the serpent slither away,
shed its skin of falsehood,
and become the dust at my feet.

I trust the earth to hold me.
I trust myself to stand.

1.3. I Am Here

(*Affirming stability and presence*)

I am not the whispers of yesterday,
nor the worry of tomorrow.
I am the breath between—
full, present, *whole*.
I have touched the depths of the unknown,
stumbled through shadows and silence,
but here I stand—
unshaken, unafraid, *unbreakable*.
The sky does not ask permission to open.
The sun does not seek approval to shine.
And I, too, will take up space,
will plant myself firm and say—

*"I am here.
I am enough.
I belong."*

P.S.: To exist fully is an act of defiance. Do not shrink. Do not waver. The world has been waiting for you to claim your place.

Part II. Sacral Chakra (Svadhishthana) – The Flow

Symbol: 6-petalled lotus, crescent moon, interlocking circles

Color: Orange

Element: Water

Location: Lower abdomen

Function: Governs emotions, creativity, and relationships

Blocked Symptoms: Emotional instability, guilt, lack of creativity

Balanced State: Joy, passion, creativity, emotional balance

Verses:

2.1 Who Were You Before the World Told You – *Reclaiming your true self beyond fear and conditioning.*

2.2 Embers of Desire – *Navigating passion without losing oneself.*

2.3 I Feel, I Create – *Harnessing emotions for transformation.*

2.1. Who Were You Before the World Told You?

(Reclaiming your true self beyond fear and conditioning)

Before shame traced its name upon your skin,
before silence swallowed your laughter,
before fear whispered,
who were you?
Did your hands mold dreams from clay,
weave wonder into the wind,
paint the sky with the fire of your longing?
Did you dance without asking permission,
love without measuring the cost,
speak without swallowing yourself whole?

What if you returned to that place?
What if you let the river inside you rise,
not to drown you,
but to set you free?

P.S.: You were born to create, to feel, to flow. The world did not give you this power—so do not ask it for permission to reclaim it.

2.2. Embers of Desire

(Navigating passion without losing oneself)

There is a fire in me,
a hunger woven into my bones,
a whisper in my blood
calling me towards something more.
Desire flickers like an ember—
a spark of longing,
a glimpse of the infinite,
the restless ache of creation.
I have chased it through the night,
let it consume reason and restraint,
only to learn that wildfire
leaves nothing but ash
if left untended.
So I cradle it carefully,
feed it just enough air
to keep it alive,
not enough to let it devour me.
Passion is not the storm,

but the steady flame,
burning bright without burning away.

I do not fear the fire within me.
I have learned to hold it well.

P.S.: Passion is sacred. Let it guide you, but never let it
rule you. Burn steady, not reckless.

2.3. I Feel, I Create

(Harnessing emotions for transformation)

My hands are rivers,
my heart is fire,
my soul is the space between—
endless, shifting, alive.
I take the ache in my chest
and turn it into color,
into music,
into words that pulse
with the rhythm of the unseen.
What I feel, I create.
What I create, I become.
I have learned that pain is not an ending,
but a doorway.
That joy is not a fleeting moment,
but a melody I can weave into being.

I am not just a witness to my emotions—
I am their sculptor.

P.S.: To feel is to be alive, but to transform those feelings
is to truly live.

Part III. Solar Plexus Chakra (Manipura) – The Fire

Symbol: 10-petalled lotus, downward-facing triangle

Color: Yellow

Element: Fire

Location: Upper abdomen

Function: Governs personal power, confidence, and self-discipline

Blocked Symptoms: Low self-esteem, insecurity, digestive issues

Balanced State: Strong willpower, confidence, motivation

Verses:

3.1 The Sun in My Belly – *Awakening inner power and confidence.*

3.2 The Alchemist's Fire – *Transforming fear into courage.*

3.3 I Will, I Shine – *Owning strength and destiny.*

3.1. The Sun in My Belly

(Awakening inner power and confidence)

There is a sun in my belly,
a golden clinker waiting to rise.
It stirs beneath my ribs,
a quiet hum of knowing,
a pulse of fire whispering—
"You are more than you have believed."
For too long, I have folded myself small,
dimmed my light to fit shadows,
quenched my fire
to keep others warm.
No more!
I let the sun expand,
stretch into my skin,
ignite the marrow of my being.
I walk taller.
I speak with thunder.
I claim my space without apology.

I am not a flicker.
I am a blaze.

P.S.: Your power was never outside of you. It was always within, waiting for you to say yes to yourself.

3.2. The Alchemist's Fire

(Transforming fear into courage)

Once, I held fear in my hands
like a brittle stone,
heavy with doubt,
sharp with hesitation.
I carried it through my days,
a quiet weight in my pocket,
a whisper in my mind—
"Not yet. Not you. Not enough."
But I have learned the alchemy of fire.
I place my fear in the flame,
watch it crack,
watch it melt,
watch it become something new.
Gold does not fear the furnace.
A phoenix does not fear the ashes.
I let the fire reshape me.
I step forward, not despite my fear,
but because of it.

And now, when the voice returns,
I answer—
"I am ready."

P.S.: Courage is not the absence of fear, but the choice to
burn brighter than your doubts.

3.3. I Will, I Shine

(Owning strength and destiny)

I have searched for permission,
waited for a sign,
held my dreams behind my teeth,
wondering if I was worthy.
And then it struck me —
I will have to rise,
not as a question,
but as an answer.
I will have to shine,
not to be seen,
but because I was born to.

This is my will.
This is my fire.

And nothing will dim me again.

P.S.: Own your light.

Part IV. Heart Chakra (Anahata) – The Bridge

Symbol: 12-petalled lotus, two intersecting triangles

Color: Green

Element: Air

Location: Center of the chest

Function: Represents love, compassion, and emotional healing

Blocked Symptoms: Fear of rejection, loneliness, jealousy

Balanced State: Love, compassion, trust, inner peace

Verses:

4.1 Thorns and Petals – *Understanding love's dual nature.*

4.2 Forgiveness as Liberation – *Healing wounds through release.*

4.3 I Love, I Am Love – *Becoming an embodiment of compassion.*

4.1. Thorns and Petals

(Understanding love's dual nature)

Love is not only the bloom,
soft and fragrant in morning light—
it is also the thorn,
sharp with truth,
demanding to be felt.
I have held love in my hands,
let its petals brush my skin,
only to flinch when its edges drew blood.
But love was never meant to be safe.
It asks for openness,
even when the wind is cold.
It asks for trust,
even when hands have known harm.
And so, I do not curse the thorn—
I learn to hold it gently.

For love is not a promise of ease,
but the courage to embrace

both its beauty and its ache.

P.S.: Love is not perfect, nor painless. But even the thorns serve a purpose—protecting what is sacred within.

4.2. Forgiveness as Liberation

(Healing wounds through release)

I have carried anger like a stone,
fingers clenched around its weight,
believing that holding it
made me stronger,
made me safe.
But the stone grew heavier,
dragging me into the past,
turning my hands cold and tired.
I thought forgiveness was surrender—
a yielding, a forgetting.
But it is neither.
It is the moment I set the stone down,
not for them, but for me.
It is the opening of clenched fists,
the unclasping of a locked heart,
the first breath after too many held in.

Forgiveness does not erase the wound.
It simply stops me from wounding myself again.

P.S.: Forgiveness is not a gift to the one who hurt you—it
is the freedom you give yourself.

4.3. I Love, I Am Love

(Becoming an embodiment of compassion)

Love is not something I seek,
not something I wait for,
not something I must be given to be whole.
Love is the river within me,
the thread that weaves me into the world,
the quiet knowing
that I am already enough.
I do not love because I must,
nor because I am asked—
I love because I *am*.
It pours from me,
like light from the sun,
like warmth from the earth,
needing no validation,
needing no return.

I am love,

and because of that,
I am free.

P.S.: Love is not outside of you. It is the essence of who
you are.

Part V. Throat Chakra (Vishuddha) – The Voice

Symbol: 16-petalled lotus, inverted triangle with circle

Color: Blue

Element: Ether/Space

Location: Throat

Function: Governs communication, truth, and self-expression

Blocked Symptoms: Fear of speaking, shyness, dishonesty, throat issues

Balanced State: Clear communication, confidence, truthfulness

Verses:

5.1 Words Like Rivers – *Expressing truth with clarity.*

5.2 The Fire in My Breath – *Speaking as an act of courage and transformation.*

5.3 I Speak, I Am Heard – *From silence to self-expression in its purest form—joy, creativity, and authenticity.*

5.1. Words Like Rivers

(*Expressing truth with clarity*)

Some speak to fill the silence,
to scatter words like pebbles on pavement,
never minding where they land.
But words, when spoken with care,
are like rivers—
flowing with purpose,
shaping the land they touch.
A single truth, well-placed,
can turn stone to sand,
can carve new paths,
can quench a thirsty soul.
So I do not rush my voice.
I let it move with intention,
clear, steady, alive.

For words that wander may be heard,
but words that flow *are understood*.

5.2. The Fire in My Breath

(Speaking as an act of courage and transformation)

There was a time I held my words back,
afraid they might spark a wildfire,
afraid of the heat they carried.
But silence, too, can burn.
It scorches the soul,
leaving behind only the ashes
of unspoken truths.
So I breathe deep.
I let my words rise,
not as destruction,
but as light,
as warmth,
as the flame that was never meant to die out.

I do not fear my voice anymore.
It is not a blaze set loose—
it is the fire that keeps me alive.

P.S.: The fire within you is not meant to be extinguished —only guided.

5.3. I Speak, I Am Heard

I sing—not to be heard,
not to be praised,
but simply because I *must.*
My voice is not just words.
It is laughter unfurling.
It is the cry of my spirit.
It is a melody too sacred to keep inside.

So I let it rise,
as natural as breath,
as free as sky.

P.S.: Your voice is more than just speech—it is the song
of your existence. Let it be sung.

Part VI. Third Eye Chakra (Ajna) – The Sight

Symbol: 2-petalled lotus, inverted triangle within a circle

Color: Indigo

Element: Light

Location: Between the eyebrows

Function: Controls intuition, wisdom, and perception

Blocked Symptoms: Lack of clarity, poor intuition, indecisiveness, headaches

Balanced State: High intuition, insight, mental clarity, spiritual awareness

Verses:

6.1 The Eye That Sees Within – *Awakening intuition.*

6.2 Mirrors of Illusion – *Discerning truth from deception.*

6.3 I See, I Know – *Attaining wisdom beyond the physical.*

6.1. The Eye That Sees Within

(Awakening intuition)

Not all vision comes through the eyes.
Some truths arrive in the hush of silence,
in the knowing before the knowing,
in the voice that whispers beneath the noise.
I have searched outside for answers,
chased shadows,
mistook reflections for reality.
But the map was never out there—
it was etched into my bones,
written in the rhythm of my breath.

To see is not to look.
It is to close my eyes
and listen.

6.2. Mirrors of Illusion

(Discerning truth from deception)

The world is a hall of mirrors,
bending light,
shaping shadows,
showing me not what *is*,
but what I am willing to believe.
I have followed illusions,
chased mirages of certainty,
mistaken comfort for truth.
But mirrors do not hold answers—
they only reflect the mind that gazes into them.
So I step beyond the glass,
beyond the shifting shapes of fear and desire,
into the stillness where truth stands bare,
unmoving, unafraid.
I do not trust the mirror.
I trust the eyes that see beyond it.

6.3. I See, I Know

(Attaining wisdom beyond the physical)

There is sight, and then there is knowing—
one bound to the eyes,
the other to the soul.
I do not need proof to understand.
I do not need permission to trust
what I already feel beneath my skin.
And so, I trust.
I see not just with my eyes,
but with the light behind them.

I see.
I know.

Part VII. Crown Chakra (Sahasrara) – The Awakening

Symbol: 1,000-petalled lotus, inverted triangle

Color: Violet/white

Element: Consciousness

Location: Top of the head

Function: Represents spiritual connection and enlightenment

Blocked Symptoms: Disconnection, depression, lack of purpose

Balanced State: Spiritual awakening, peace, wisdom, deep universal connection

Verses:

7.1 A Thousand Petals Unfold – *Experiencing spiritual awakening.*

7.2 The Last Question – *When every answer fades, what remains?*

7.3 I Am, I Am Not – *Dissolving ego into pure consciousness.*

7.1. A Thousand Petals Unfold

(*Experiencing spiritual awakening*)

I searched for divinity in distant places,
in temples of stone,
in scriptures bound by time,
in the voices of those who claimed to know.
But the sacred was never beyond me—
it was waiting in the silence,
in the breath between thoughts,
in the stillness where I became
everything and nothing at once.
Awakening is not an arrival,
not a summit to be reached—
it is a flower opening to the light,

until there is nothing left to do
but bloom.

7.2. The Last Question

(When every answer fades, what remains?)

I chased knowledge like a moth to flame,
gathering truths only to watch them flicker.
Each answer I held
became ash in my hands,
each certainty crumbled into dust.
Still, I climbed—
higher, deeper, beyond,
where thought dissolves into silence,
where even the questioner is questioned.
And there,
at the quiet horizon of mind,
the last question awaited.
I reached for it,
expecting revelation,
but it did not speak.
Instead, it turned to me,
eyes deep as the spaces between stars,
and whispered—

"Who is asking?"

In that instant,
I became the answer,
and the question
was no more.

P.S.: The last question is the one that makes you realize
you never needed an answer.

7.3. I Am, I Am Not

(Dissolving ego into pure consciousness)

I spent my life defining myself—
by name, by past,
by the roles I played,
by the stories I clung to.
But when I let go,
when I stopped holding onto what I *thought* I was,
I felt the truth waiting beneath it all—
I am the wave,
but I am also the ocean.
I am the breath,
but I am also the wind.
I exist,
but I do not need to be separate.
There is no *I*,
and yet—
I am.

Awakening the Chakras...
Reflections & Rituals

A Note to the Reader

As you journey through this section, take a moment to pause, reflect, and connect with yourself on a deeper level. The chakras are not just energy centers; they are gateways to self-awareness, healing, and transformation. Each one holds a unique key to unlocking different aspects of your mind, body, and spirit.

The following pages invite you to explore these energies through **introspection, rituals**, and **mindful practices**. You may choose to move through them in order or intuitively focus on the chakra that calls to you most. Allow yourself to **breathe, feel**, and **embrace the process**, knowing that growth is not about perfection but about presence.

Take your time. Sit with the questions. Try the practices.

Root Chakra (Muladhara) – Grounding & Stability

Reflection:

✦ What makes you feel safe, secure, and grounded?

✦ How do you respond to fear and uncertainty?

Rituals:

• **Earthing**: Walk barefoot on grass or soil.
• **Root Affirmations**: Repeat: "I am safe. I am grounded."
• **Root Nourishment**: Eat red foods like beets, tomatoes, and apples.

Sacral Chakra (Svadhisthana) – Creativity & Emotions

Reflection:

✦ How do you express creativity in your life?

✦ Do you allow yourself to experience pleasure without guilt?

Rituals:
- **Creative Flow**: Engage in art, dance, or music.
- **Water Ritual**: Take a mindful bath or spend time near water.
- **Sacral Nourishment**: Eat orange foods like carrots, mangoes, and oranges.

Solar Plexus Chakra (Manipura) – Confidence & Power

Reflection:

✦ Do you trust yourself and your decisions?

✦ How do you handle criticism and setbacks?

Rituals:

• **Fire Meditation**: Visualize a golden sun at your core and meditate.

• **Power Pose**: Repeat: "I am strong. I trust myself."

• **Solar Nourishment**: Eat yellow foods like bananas, corn, and turmeric.

Heart Chakra (Anahata) – Love & Compassion

Reflection:

✦ Do you give and receive love freely?

✦ Are there past hurts that need healing?

Rituals:

• **Gratitude Practice**: Write down three things you love about yourself.

• **Love-Kindness Meditation**: Close your eyes and repeat: "May I be happy. May I be healthy. May I be at peace." Then extend the same wishes to others.

• **Heart Nourishment**: Eat green foods like spinach, kiwi, and avocado.

Throat Chakra (Vishuddha) – Communication & Truth

Reflection:

✦ Do you speak your truth with confidence?

✦ How do you handle difficult conversations?

Rituals:

• **Conscious Listening**: Practice mindful listening by fully focusing on someone's words without interrupting.

• **Truth Writing:** Free-write for 10 minutes without self-editing.

• **Throat Nourishment:** Drink herbal teas and eat blueberries.

Third Eye Chakra (Ajna) – Intuition & Wisdom

Reflection:

✦ Do you trust your inner guidance?

✦ How do you connect with your intuition?

Rituals:

• **Visualization:** Picture an indigo light at your forehead expanding outward.

• **Dream Awareness:** Observe and reflect on recurring dreams.

• **Third Eye Nourishment:** Eat dark foods like blackberries, grapes, and cacao.

Crown Chakra (Sahasrara) – Spiritual Connection & Enlightenment

Reflection:

✦ What does spirituality mean to you?

✦ Do you feel connected to something greater than yourself?

Rituals:

- **Silence & Stillness:** Spend time in quiet meditation.
- **Gratitude for the Universe:** Reflect on what you're grateful for beyond the material world.
- **Crown Nourishment:** Drink plenty of water and eat light, plant-based foods.

The Next Step: Living in Alignment

✦ My biggest takeaway from this journey:

✦ The chakra I feel most aligned with right now:

✦ The chakra that needs the most attention:

✦ One daily practice I will commit to for balance:

✦ My personal affirmation to guide my path:

Parting Thoughts...

Spirituality is not a straight path but a spiral. You will return to the same lessons, the same energies, the same emotions—but each time with deeper awareness.

Keep spiraling upward, keep unraveling the truth of who you are!

www.ingramcontent.com/pod-product-compliance
Lightning Source LLC
La Vergne TN
LVHW021212200726
843509LV00012B/1424